3-D THRILLERS!

W9-BLZ-396

SPACE

and the Wonders of the Solar System

PAUL HARRISON

SCHOLASTIC

New York • Toronto • London • Auckland
Sydney • Mexico City • New Delhi • Hong Kong

BIG BANG!

Most scientists think the universe began about 14 billion years ago with a huge explosion called the Big Bang. At first, the universe was just gas. Then, over billions of years, stars, planets, and galaxies began to form.

GALAXIES are huge groups of STARS that come in three basic shapes—spiral, elliptical, and irregular.

◀ **Big crunch!** The universe contains billions of galaxies that are all moving away from one another. That means the universe is still expanding. Scientists don't know if the universe will continue to expand or if it will start to shrink. If it does start to shrink, then billions of years from now it could squash back together. Scientists call this the Big Crunch.

▲ Light-years away

The universe is so big that it's just not possible to measure distances in space the same way as we do on Earth. Instead, astronomers use light-years. One light-year is the distance that light travels in one Earth year. That's 5.9 trillion miles (9.5 trillion km)! The Andromeda galaxy is the closest to our own galaxy, the Milky Way. It's about 2.5 million light-years away.

▼ Shining star

Our Sun is just one of the many billions of stars that are in space. The reason it looks so different from all the other stars in the sky is because Earth is so much closer to it. Stars are gigantic balls of gas that come in different sizes and temperatures.

SPINNING

Everything in space is spinning around. All the planets, moons, stars, and even the galaxies are spinning! The solar system is what we call the Sun and everything else in space that travels around it. Astronomers think there are at least eight planets traveling around the Sun, and one of these is planet Earth.

▼ In a spin

The Sun is at the center of the solar system, and all the planets travel around it counterclockwise, following invisible paths called orbits. At the same time as each planet orbits around the Sun, it also spins on itself, like a spinning top. Apart from the Sun and the planets, the solar system includes moons, meteoroids, asteroids, and comets.

AROUND

Polish astronomer Nicolaus COPERNICUS (1473–1543) was the first person to claim that EARTH moves around the SUN.

◀ Milky Way

A galaxy is a cluster of hundreds of billions of stars, dust, gases, and other space objects. Our solar system is part of the Milky Way galaxy. From Earth, the Milky Way appears as a soft glowing band of light in the sky. In ancient times, people thought it looked like a stream of milk in the night sky, which is how it got its name.

Fiery rocks ▶

A comet is a ball of ice and dust that orbits the Sun. As a comet comes close to the Sun, the Sun's heat turns some of its ice into gas, making a long, fiery tail in the sky.

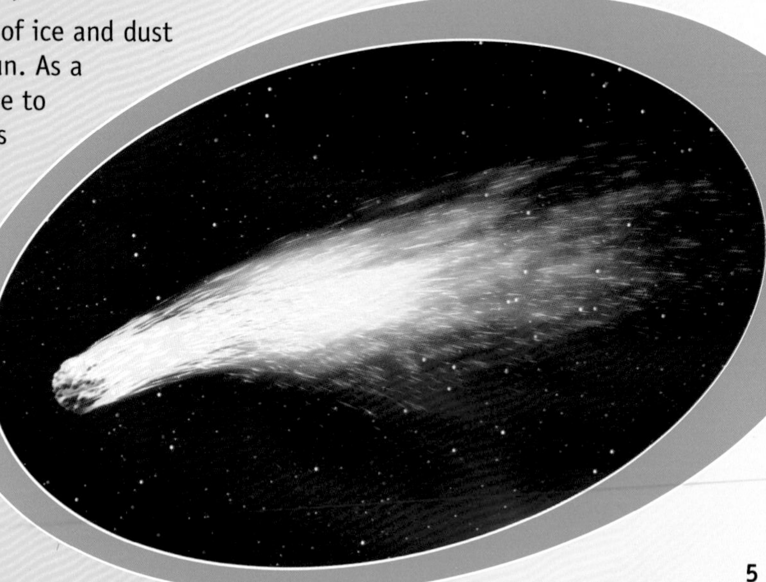

THE ORIGINAL

Our Sun gives us heat, light, and energy. Without it, there would be no life on Earth. It would be so cold that no living creature could survive and Earth would be frozen.

▼ Blackout

If the Moon passes between Earth and the Sun, a shadow is cast over a small part of Earth, making it dark. This is called a solar eclipse. In a total solar eclipse, you can't see the Sun at all, but you can still see a ring of light around the Moon from the Sun.

▲ Hot giant

Earth seems like a pretty big place to us, but not compared to the Sun. The Sun is a whopping 333,000 times Earth's mass and 109 times as wide. In fact, you could fit one million Earths inside it. Even so, the Sun is actually a medium-sized star. There are countless stars in the universe far bigger than our Sun.

SUPERSTAR!

▼ Dazzling display

The surface of the Sun is 60 times hotter than boiling water and bubbles like a giant soup. Loops and solar flares of scalding gas are often flung up from the surface, like a giant fireworks display. There are some darker patches on the Sun, known as sunspots, which are where the gas is cooler than the rest of the Sun.

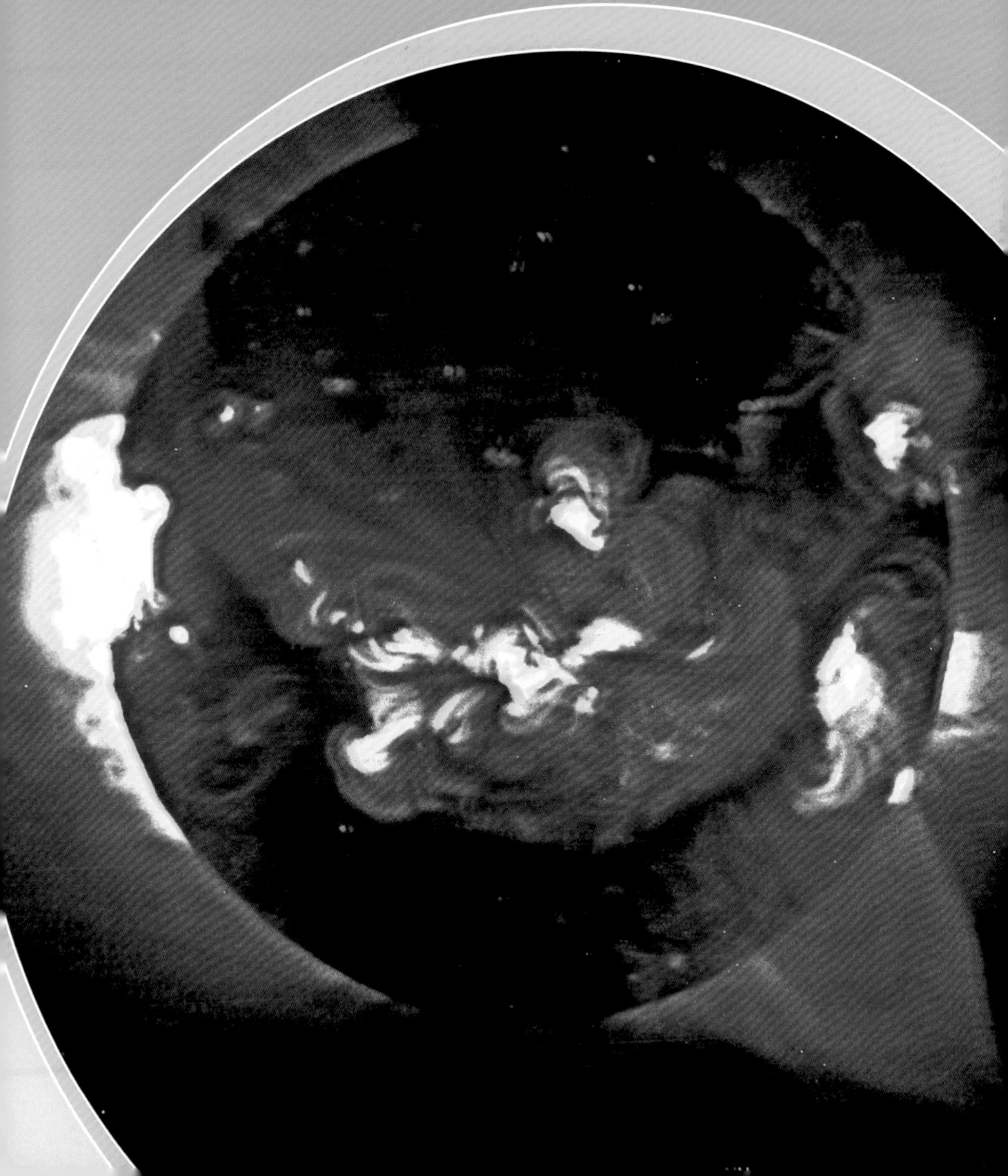

HOME SWEET

Earth is our home and the third planet from the Sun. It's just the right distance from the Sun for living things to exist and the only place in the solar system known to have life. A layer of air surrounds Earth that allows people and animals to breathe.

▲ Location, location

Location is everything. If Earth were any closer to the Sun, it would be too hot; any farther away, and it would be too cold. Even though there are some really hot areas on Earth, such as the Sahara Desert, and icy areas, such as the poles, our planet is very liveable. The temperature on Earth is just right for water to be liquid.

◀ Blue planet

Oceans of water cover more than 70 percent of Earth's surface. From space, our planet looks blue, with swirling white clouds made of droplets of water.

HOME

▼ Moon walk

The Moon is Earth's closest neighbor and the only other place in the solar system where humans have walked. In 1969, Neil Armstrong of Wapakoneta, Ohio, commander of the Apollo 11 mission, became the first person to walk on the Moon. Only eleven other people have done the same.

THE ROCKIES

Earth and its three closest neighbor planets—Mercury, Venus, and Mars—are known as the rocky planets. They are all made mostly of rock and are similar in size—but that's where their similarities end. These planets couldn't be more different.

VENUS can be seen just after sunset, called the **EVENING STAR**, and just before sunrise, called the **MORNING STAR**.

◀ Hot and cold

At a distance of 36 million miles (58 million km), Mercury is the closest planet to the Sun and the smallest planet in the solar system. Mercury also has the biggest temperature range of all the planets. During the day, temperatures can reach a blistering 801°F (427°C), and at night a bitterly cold -279°F (-173°C). In 1974, the unmanned space probe Mariner 10 sent photographs of Mercury back to Earth. The images show that its surface is covered in craters, like the Moon.

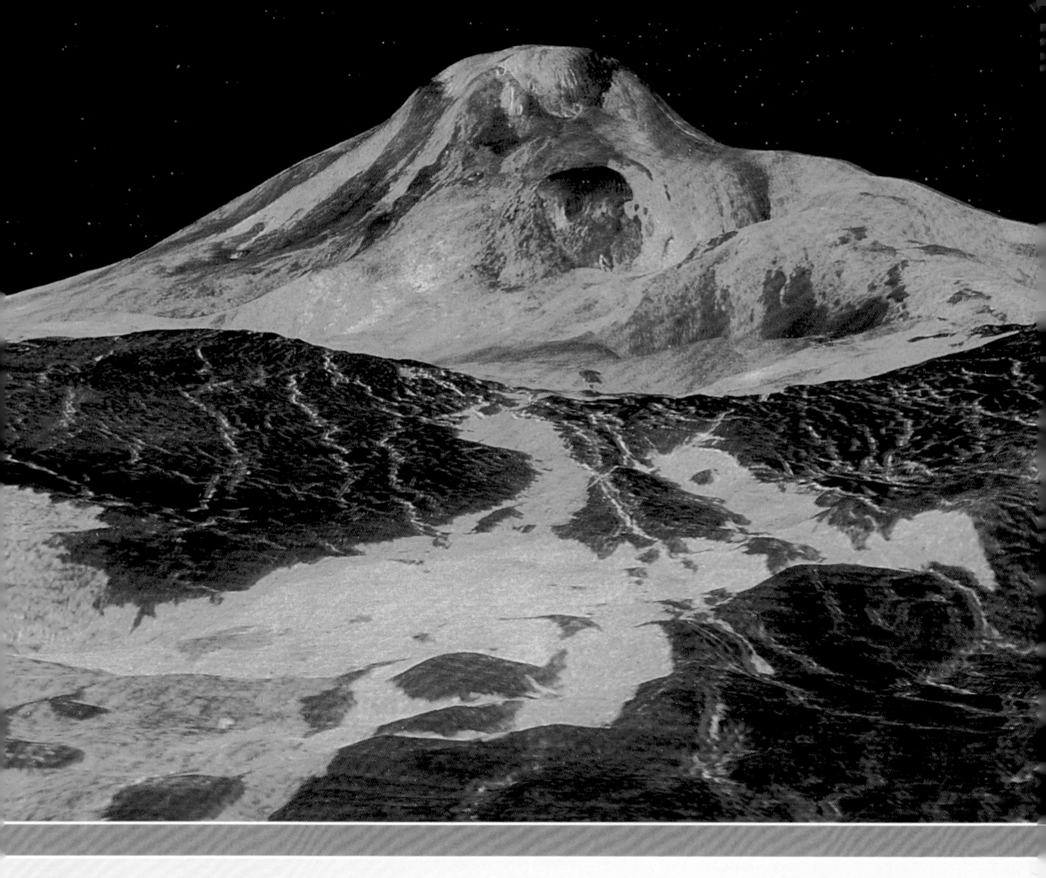

▲ Acid clouds

Venus is the second planet from the Sun. The surface of Venus is hidden by a blanket of thick, swirling clouds that contain acid. These clouds trap the Sun's heat, making Venus even hotter than Mercury. Temperatures here can reach up to 864°F (462°C).

Red Planet ▶

Mars is the farthest rocky planet from the Sun. It's known as the Red Planet because, from Earth, it looks reddish in the sky. That's because its soil contains iron, which rusts and turns the surface of the planet red.

GAS GIANTS

The solar system's giants are Jupiter and Saturn. Jupiter is the biggest planet in the solar system, with Saturn coming in at a close second. Both planets are mainly made up of gases, and each has a number of moons that revolve around it.

▼ Big red spot

Jupiter is the fifth planet from the Sun and is more than 11 times wider than Earth! The Great Red Spot is a huge storm that is raging in Jupiter's thick clouds. It was first noticed by astronomers over 300 years ago!

◀ Many moons

Jupiter has 64 moons, but four are famous for being the size of small planets. Io, shown here, is the most volcanic place in the solar system. Fiery volcanoes cover Io's landscape and massive lava flows spread out over enormous distances.

▼ Rings

Saturn is the second-largest planet in the solar system. Like Jupiter, it is covered by clouds and little is known of what lies beneath. Saturn is best known for the brilliant set of rings that circle it. These are made up of millions of chunks of icy rock, each one moving in its own orbit around the planet. Some of the chunks are as small as a dust particle, while others are the size of a car. They reflect the Sun's light, which makes them shine brightly.

Saturn is the LIGHTEST planet in the solar system. It would FLOAT on water if there were an ocean large enough to hold it.

DISTANT

The outermost planets in the solar system are Uranus and Neptune. Only a little of the Sun's heat reaches out this far, so these planets are icy and cold. Much of what we know about them was learned only recently.

▲ Ice giant

Uranus lies so far away from the Sun that it is always colder than the coldest winter on Earth. Uranus also spins on its side, so instead of spinning like a top, it rolls along, like a marble, as it orbits the Sun.

◄ Blue world

Neptune was named after the Roman god of the sea because of its rich blue color. Blue clouds streaked with white cover its surface. Neptune has the fastest winds in the solar system, which whip around the planet at speeds of up to 700 miles (1,100 km) per hour. The Great Dark Spot, seen left, is an enormous storm in Neptune's clouds.

RELATIVES

▼ What happened to Pluto?

Scientists don't consider Pluto a planet at all, but rather a dwarf planet. That's because it's small and its orbit is irregular. Pluto is so far away that it was discovered only in 1930 by an astronomer named Clyde Tombaugh. Charon is Pluto's moon, and it is thought to be about half the size of Pluto. Together, they are sometimes called a double dwarf planet system.

PLUTO is now thought to be an object in the **KUIPER BELT**, an area of icy, dark objects beyond **NEPTUNE**.

ROCKETING

Comets, asteroids, and meteoroids are the rock stars of space. Like the planets, they are also in orbit around the Sun. Asteroids are large chunks of rock; comets are balls of cosmic snow and ice; and meteoroids are small asteroids, some no larger than a speck of dust.

▼ Belt up

Asteroids are found in a band called the asteroid belt, between the planets Mars and Jupiter. It is thought that asteroids are chunks of rock that have been around since the formation of the solar system. These chunks did not form a planet because the gravity of nearby Jupiter was too strong. Asteroids are different sizes and most have irregular shapes. Ceres, the largest asteroid and the first to be discovered, is 580 miles (933 km) across. It is covered in large craters.

ROCKS

Tail first ▶

As a comet nears the Sun, the Sun's heat turns some of its ice into gas. This makes a long, bright tail in the sky that always points away from the Sun. In 1997, the comet Hale-Bopp appeared and was so bright in the night sky that it could be seen without a telescope.

▲ Colossal crater

Once a meteoroid enters Earth's atmosphere, it's known as a meteor. Most meteors are small and burn up in the atmosphere. But occasionally, large ones hit Earth and these are called meteorites. The meteorite that made this huge crater in Arizona was probably 80 feet (24 m) wide.

STARRY NIGHT

How many stars can you see in the night sky? Even on the clearest, darkest night it's only possible to see around 3,000 stars. But there are said to be more stars in the universe than there are grains of sand on all the beaches on Earth.

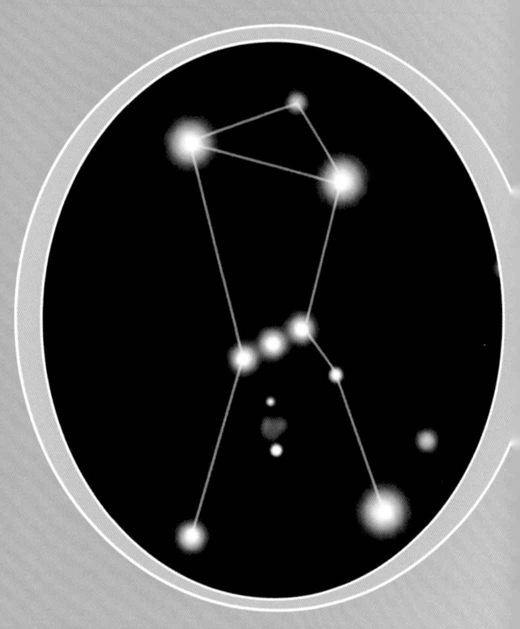

▲ Hunter

Years ago, our ancestors looked up at the stars and drew imaginary lines between them, creating pictures called constellations. Orion, also known as the hunter, is a very large, bright constellation.

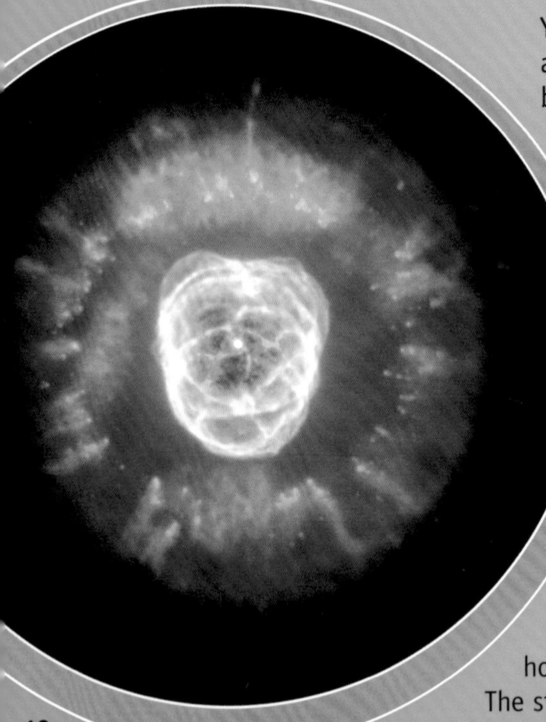

◄ Star nursery

A star has a life cycle of birth, life, and death. It can live for millions or even billions of years, but it does not shine forever. A star is born inside a cloud of gas and dust called a nebula. Within the nebula, clumps of gas and dust shrink into a ball that becomes smaller and hotter. The center of the ball becomes hot enough for the gas to make energy. The star then starts to shine steadily.

▼ Supernova

The larger the star, the brighter it burns, and the shorter it lives. A star with a mass many times greater than that of our Sun may die in a violent explosion called a supernova. As it blows apart, it shines brighter than a billion Suns. The remains of the star shrink to a hot ball called a neutron star.

For many years, people have used the NORTH STAR to guide them at night because it always shows which way is NORTH.

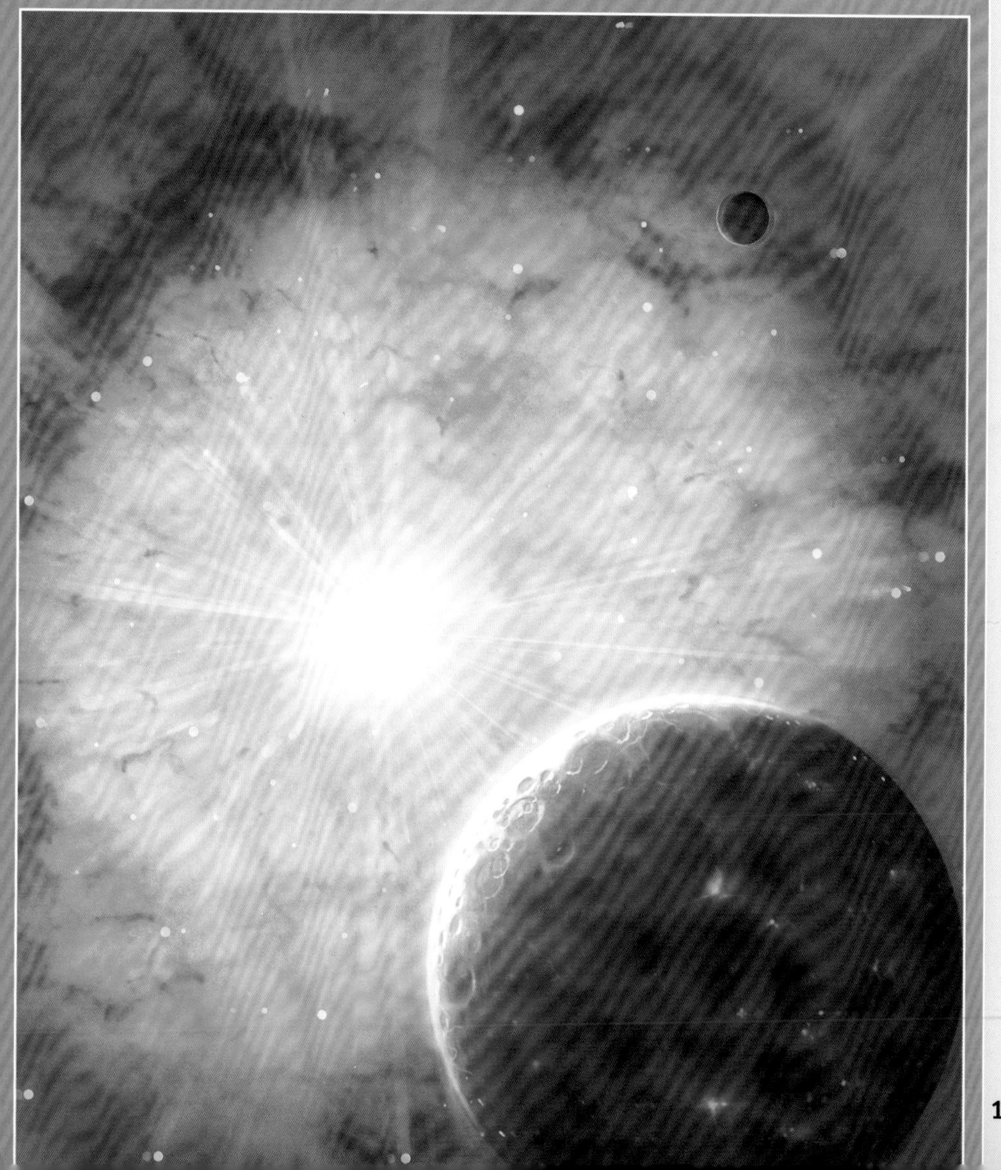

EYES ON THE

Telescopes allow astronomers to see objects that are so far away, their light takes billions of years just to reach us! Many of these telescopes use huge mirrors to gather light that is then focused by a lens. Others, such as radio telescopes, pick up radiation from space, including radio waves, X-rays, and ultraviolet rays.

The HUBBLE SPACE TELESCOPE is so powerful, it can spot a coin over 400 miles (700 km) away.

▼ On a high

Modern telescopes are often grouped together in buildings called observatories. These are usually built high on the tops of mountains, where there is less interference from pollution and the light from distant stars and galaxies is less blurred.

SKIES

Hubble ▶

In 1990, the Hubble telescope was launched into space. It orbits Earth around 353 miles (569 km) above its surface. Not only is it closer to the stars, but also pollution and clouds cannot affect its view. So far, Hubble has sent back close-up images of most of the planets and moons in the solar system, and images of faraway galaxies that had never been seen before.

Super sensors ▶

Distant objects can sometimes be detected using separate radio dishes that work together. The Very Large Array in New Mexico is made up of 27 radio telescopes, and each one is 82 feet (25 m) across.

INFINITY AND

When astronomers want to get a really close look at an object out in space, they send up a space probe. A space probe doesn't carry astronauts on board. It's a spacecraft that sends pictures and information back to Earth for astronomers to study.

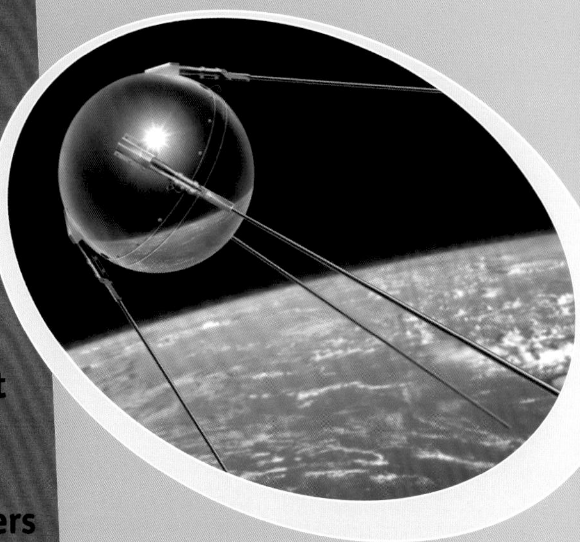

▲Around and around

In 1957, Sputnik was the first satellite ever to be launched. It sent out a simple radio signal so that it could be tracked on its orbit around Earth. Now there are thousands of artificial satellites. Some are weather satellites that can warn people if a hurricane is approaching. Others are communications satellites that send TV and phone signals all around the world.

◄ Hard landing

Some space probes, such as Deep Impact, are designed to crash into a space object. Part of Deep Impact was sent to crash into a comet called Tempel 1 so that scientists could find out what the comet was made of. This type of crash is called a hard landing!

BEYOND!

The MARS ROVERS were meant to last only 90 days, but Spirit lasted until 2010 and Opportunity is still working and exploring!

▼ Wheely useful

In 2003, NASA's Mars Exploration Rover mission sent two robotic probes, called Spirit and Opportunity, to Mars's surface. The six-wheeled vehicles, also called Mars Rovers, could move around the planet like remote-controlled cars. They found evidence that water used to flow on Mars and sent details back to Earth of volcanoes, lava plains, and huge canyons. They also tested samples of Martian soil and although these were rich in iron, no signs of life were found.

TO BOLDLY GO

In 1961, Yuri Gagarin, a Russian cosmonaut (the Russian word for astronaut), became the first person to go into space and the first to orbit Earth. After this, a "space race" began between the Soviet Union and the United States to see who would be the first to land a human being on the Moon.

Blast off ▶

The first problem with space exploration is overcoming Earth's gravity. To do that, you need speed, and to get that kind of speed, you need a rocket! The biggest rocket ever built was Saturn V. It was as tall as a 36-story building and sent three US astronauts to the Moon. Their spacecraft was called Apollo 11, and it took three days for the astronauts to reach the Moon. One astronaut remained in the Apollo spacecraft while the other two flew down to the Moon inside a lunar lander named the *Eagle*. They spent a day exploring the Moon's surface before flying back up to the spacecraft and returning to Earth.

▲ Home, sweet home

Sending people into space is very expensive, so it makes sense to keep them up there for as long as possible. A space station is a home for astronauts and is a kind of floating laboratory. The International Space Station, which is in orbit around Earth, is a joint venture between 16 different countries. It is also the biggest artificial object in space.

Recycled ►

The space shuttle is the first, and so far only, reusable spacecraft that can fly back and forth into space. The space shuttle is also a highly complex machine. It has several parts: an orbiter that carries the astronauts into space, a fuel tank, and two booster rockets.

MYSTERIOUS

There are lots of things that scientists still don't know about space. For example, what does it look like inside a black hole? Is it possible to travel through space and time? What is it that holds the universe together? Scientists are still searching for answers to all these questions and many more.

At the center of the MILKY WAY galaxy there is a supermassive BLACK HOLE called SAGITTARIUS A.

▼Black hole

After a supernova explosion, a massive star may fall in on itself, or collapse, creating a black hole. Near a black hole, stars are torn apart and gas is sucked in. A black hole's powerful gravity even sucks in light.

SPACE

▲ Wormholes

Some scientists think there might be tunnels in space that lead to different parts of the universe—or even back in time! These tunnels are known as wormholes, and are based on the theory that a person could enter a wormhole and pop out in a faraway part of space. Scientists know that gravity can affect time so, in theory, it is possible to travel through time.

Dark matter ▶

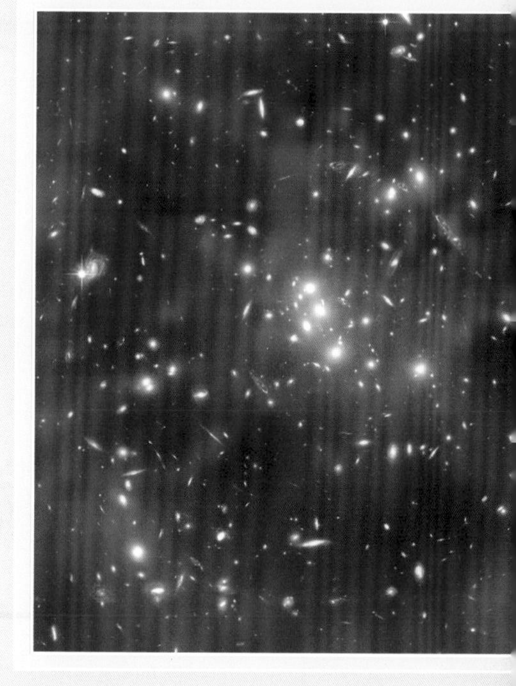

All the stars, planets, and other space objects that scientists have detected using powerful telescopes make up only about 5 percent of the universe. The rest is called dark energy, or dark matter. Scientists know that it exists, even though they cannot see it, because it has a gravitational effect on the stars and galaxies. They just don't know what it is!

THE FUTURE

Our achievements in space are just the beginning. There are some amazing plans for the future of space exploration, which include a permanent base on the Moon, vacations in space, and even a visit to Mars!

▼ Space vacation

In 2001, Dennis Tito became the first space tourist when he paid to fly on a Russian rocket and spend time on the International Space Station. The trip was literally out of this world, and so was the price—it cost him $20 million.

▼ Moon base

The US space agency NASA has plans to build a base on the Moon that would be both a laboratory and a launchpad for future space missions. Gravity is weaker on the Moon than it is on Earth, so it would be easier, and cheaper, for spacecraft to take off from there.

OF SPACE

▲ Galactic fantastic

Virgin Galactic is a company with plans to provide space flights for ordinary people—although at a price of $200,000 per person with a $20,000 deposit! The craft will carry six passengers and two pilots, and will overlap Earth's atmosphere at 70,000 feet (21,000 m) above the surface. Passengers will even experience a period of weightlessness for part of their journey.

By 2100, scientists hope to have worked out the plans to build an enormous STARSHIP the size of a city that will fly through space for a HUNDRED years!

SPACE FACTS

Now that you've traveled through the solar system and learned about all the amazing stars and galaxies, and how scientists are exploring the universe, you probably think you know it all. Not quite! Here are even more amazing space facts.

▼ Mission to Saturn

Since 2004, the *Cassini* spacecraft has been orbiting Saturn. It has sent lots of information back about the planet's magnificent rings and its amazing moons, especially Titan. *Cassini* has revealed that beneath Titan's thick, smog-filled atmosphere, there are vast lakes, stretches of sand dunes, and an ocean of liquid water. *Cassini* is expected to continue its mission until September 2017.

▲ Floating around

In a spacecraft, there is no gravity, so people and things float around. To stay still, astronauts have to push their feet into special loops attached to the spacecraft. To sleep, they lie in space beds that are fixed to the walls.

▼ Probing Mars

Since 1965, more than 40 space probes have been sent to Mars. A new mission will land in August 2012 that includes a new rover called Curiosity. This clever rover will roam the planet, zapping at rocks with a laser! Then it will test the rocks and soil to see if life could ever exist, or has ever existed, on the Red Planet.

This edition created in 2012 by
Arcturus Publishing Limited, 26/27 Bickels Yard,
151–153 Bermondsey Street, London SE1 3HA

Copyright © 2012 by Arcturus Publishing Limited

All rights reserved. Published by Scholastic Inc., *Publishers since 1920*. SCHOLASTIC and associated logos are trademarks and/or registered trademarks of Scholastic Inc.

No part of this publication may be reproduced, stored in a retrieval system, or transmitted in any form or by any means, electronic, mechanical, photocopying, recording, or otherwise, without written permission of the publisher. For information regarding permission, write to Scholastic Inc., Attention: Permissions Department, 557 Broadway, New York, NY 10012.

ISBN 978-0-545-46554-0

10 9 8 7 6 5 4 3 2 1 12 13 14 15 16

Printed in Malaysia 106

First Scholastic edition, September 2012

ARCTURUS CREDITS
Author: Paul Harrison
Editors: Samantha Williams and Kate Overy
Designer: Tania Rösler
Illustrator (glasses): Ian Thompson

PICTURE CREDITS
Corbis: p. 5 bottom, p. 6 top, p. 17 center, p. 21 bottom, p. 23, p. 25 bottom, p. 27 top, p. 28 center
Galaxy Picture Library: p. 3 top, p. 17 top
Genesis Space Photo Library: p. 11 top, p. 12 center, p. 32
Jisas Lockheed: p. 7
Luke Dodd: p. 5 top
NASA: p. 8 top, p. 8 bottom, p. 10, p. 11 bottom, p. 12 bottom, p. 13, p. 14 bottom, p. 18 bottom, p. 21 top, p. 24, p. 26, p. 27 bottom, p. 28 bottom, p. 31 top
Reuters: p. 29
Robert Harding Picture Library: p. 6 bottom, p. 9
Science Photo Library: p. 14 top, p. 15, p. 16, p. 18 top, p. 19, p. 20, p. 22 top and bottom, p. 31 bottom
Shutterstock: title, p. 2, p. 3 bottom, p. 4, p. 25 top, p. 30

3-D images produced by Pinsharp 3-D Graphics